I0169537

DICTIONARY OF ASTROLOGICAL TERMS AND EXPLANATIONS

★

A Brief Glossary and Explanation
of the Technical Terms Employed

Compiled by

A. E. PARTRIDGE

Copyrighted 1933
Entered at Stationers' Hall, London, England

THE SIMPLEX PUBLISHING CO.
Box 595
Seattle, Washington

Dictionary
of
Astrological Terms

A concise and lucid explanation of the Astrological terms employed. The student should familiarize himself with these definitions which are of primary importance in the Study of Astrology.

ALEPH. The first word in the Hebrew Alphabet, symbolized by the Constellation of Taurus ♉ the Bull.

ADJUSTED CALCULATION DATE. A date used in the Progressed Horoscope, when Planets culminate. See instructions in Technique of Astrology on how to find.

AFFLICTION. A Parallel P, Conjunction ☌, Square □ or Opposition ☍, to Mars ♂, Saturn ♄, Uranus ♅ or Neptune ♆, or a Square □ or Opposition ☍ to any of the other Planets.

AIRY SIGNS. Gemini ♊, Libra ♎, and Aquarius ♒,—the Mental Signs.

ANGELS. The Planetary Angels, certain intelligences said to rule over the Planets as follows: The Sun ☉, Michael; The Moon ☽, Gabriel; Mercury ☿, Raphael; Saturn ♄, Cassiel; Mars ♂, Samael; Jupiter ♃, Zadkiel; Venus ♀, Anad; Uranus ♅, Arvath.

ANGLES. The four Cardinal points forming the Cross—or square—also known as the Ascendant, Mid-Heaven, Descendant, and Nadir, i. e., the 1st, 4th, 7th, and 10th Houses.

APPLICATION. When one Planet applies to another. The Moon ☽ applies to all Planets, being the quickest traveller.

APOGEE. That point in the Moon's ☽ orbit which is farthest from the Earth. The Point in the Earth's orbit which is farthest from the Sun ☉. The greatest distance of any Planet or Star from the Earth.

AQUARIUS (♒). The Water Bearer. The 11th Sign of the Zodiac. It is a Fixed, Air Sign, Home of Saturn ♄ and Uranus ♅. The Sun ☉ enters Aquarius ♒ on Jan. 22.

ARIES (♈). The Ram. The first sign of the Zodiac. A Cardinal, Fire Sign, home of Mars ♂. The Sun enters Aries on March 22.

ASCENDANT. The first House, or that sign which rises at birth.

ASCENDING. When a Planet is between the 4th and 10th Houses it is always in the East and said to be ascending.

ASPECTS. The relationship one Planet or sign has to another in the Zodiac. The Ancients

4

only considered six Aspects, called the Conjunction ☌, the Sextile ✶ or 60° Degrees. The Square ☐ or 90° Degrees. The Trine △ or 120°. The Opposition ☍ or 180 Degrees. The Parallel of Declination.

ASTRALBE. An instrument for obtaining the altitude of a Planet or Star.

ASTROLOGY. The Science which points out the working of a definite law, through which Humanity can realize that as ye sow so shall ye reap. It was a secret Science in the East and its true teachings have ever remained so to this day. The abuse of this Science by those who practiced it solely for personal gain brought about so much corruption that the key was lost for many centuries and is only now being recovered by earnest students.

BENEFICS. Venus ♀ and Jupiter ♃ when not afflicted are always good. The Benefic Aspects are the Trine △, Sextile ✶, and Semi-Sextile ⚹. The Parallel and Conjunction ☌ are only good when the Benefics are in these Aspects. Venus ♀, Jupiter ♃, and the Sun ☉ are benefic unless in bad aspect.

BESIEGED. When a Planet is between two others. If between Jupiter ♃ and Venus ♀ it is good. If between Saturn ♄ and Mars ♂ it is evil.

BESTIAL SIGNS. Aries ♈, Taurus ♉, Leo♌, Sagittarius ♐, and Capricorn ♑. If many Planets are posited in these Signs, the natures are said to partake more of the lower than the higher qualities.

5

BICORPOREAL SIGNS. Gemini ♊, Sagittarius ♐ and Pisces ♓, so called because they are double Bodied Signs.

CADENT. Those Houses which fall from angles. The 3rd, 6th, 9th and 12th Houses are Cadent and said to be weak.

CANCER (♋). The Crab. The 4th Sign of the Zodiac. It is Cardinal, Tropical, Home of the Moon. The Sun ☉ enters Cancer ♋ on June 22nd.

CAPRICORN (♑). The Goat. The 10th sign of the Zodiac. It is Cardinal, Southern, Tropical, Home of Saturn ♄. The Sun ☉ enters Capricorn ♑ on Dec. 22nd.

CARDINAL SIGNS. Aries ♈, Cancer ♋, Libra ♎, and Capricorn ♑. The 1st, 4th, 7th and 10th Houses, or the Cardinal Points, N. S. E. W.

CASTING THE NATIVITY. A term used by Astrologers, implying the necessary calculations in casting a Horoscope or Map.

CHALDEAN. The wise Men of the East and their Priests, especially famous as Astrologers.

CHANGEABLE SIGNS. Aries ♈, Cancer ♋, Libra ♎, Capricorn ♑. Known as the four Cardinal Signs.

CLIMATERICAL PERIODS. Every 7th and 9th year in a Nativity, brought about through the influence of the Moon in its position in the Radix. The Moon squares her own Place every 7th day (or 7th year Progressed), and forms a Trine every 9th day and year. These influences are important as they dominate every 7th, 9th, 14th, 18th year, and so on through life.

COMMON SIGNS. Gemini ♊, Virgo ♍, Sagittarius ♐, and Pisces ♓. Also known as Dual or Double Bodied Signs.

COMBUST. When a Planet is within 7° Deg. (some claim only 3°) of the Sun ⊙. Its influence is overcome in a measure, except in the case of Mars ♂ whose influence is intensified.

COLD PLANETS. The Moon ☽ and Saturn ♄.

COLD SIGNS. Cancer ♋ and Capricorn ♑.

COLOR OF PLANETS. The Sun ⊙, Orange; Moon ☽, green; Venus ♀, yellow; Mars ♂, red; Jupiter ♃, violet; Saturn ♄ bluish gray; Mercury ☿, royal purple; Uranus ♅, light purple with blue; Neptune ♆, very dark blue.

COLORS OF SIGNS. Aries ♈, white and red; Taurus ♉, red and yellow; Gemini ♊, purple and white; Cancer ♋, green; Leo ♌, gold and orange; Virgo ♍, brown and light blue; Libra ♎, dark crimson and pale blue; Scorpio ♏, brown and red; Sagittarius ♐, violet and green; Capricorn ♑, dark brown and grey; Aquarius ♒, light blue and yellow; Pisces ♓, white.

CONCEPTIVE SIGNS. Taurus ♉, Leo ♌, Scorpio ♏, Aquarius ♒.

CONFIGURATION. The relative position of the Planets. A term used in association with the Natal Chart when indicating the position of the Planets at birth.

CONJUNCTION (☌). When two Planets are in same degree of Longitude, or within Orb of

7

each other, they are said to be in Conjunction ☌. Thus, at the New Moon, when the Moon ☽ makes its monthly transit of the place of the Sun ☉ it is in Conjunction ☌. The Conjunction of benefic Planets is considered good, but with Mars ♂, Uranus ♅, and Saturn ♄, it is evil. The Conjunction ☌ of Mars ♂ and Venus ♀, tends to carry the mind into the lower objective, and may not be considered as evil.

CONSTELLATIONS. A group of stars within an imaginary Circle. There were forty-eight Constellations known to the Ancients, including the twelve Signs of the Zodiac.

CULMINATE. When a Planet has attained the cusp of the 10th House or Midheaven.

CUSP. The beginning, or first point of any House. The Sun ☉ is on the cusp of the 10th House at Noon.

DEBILITY. When a Planet is posited in a Sign of dissimilar nature it is considered weak or in its debility, as Mars ♂ in Taurus ♉, or Saturn ♄ in Pisces ♓.

DECANATE. A division of the Zodiacal Signs into three equal parts of ten degrees each.

DECLINATION. The distance of any Planet North or South of the Equator. The Sun ☉ is never more than 23° 28′ and reaches this point in Cancer ♋ and Capricorn ♑ each year.

DECREASING IN LIGHT. When the Moon ☽ or other Planet is passing from the opposi-

8

tion ☌ to a Conjunction of the Sun ☉ it is said to be a sign of weakness.

DECUMBITURE. A Map cast at the exact time a person is taken sick. The position of the Planets indicate the possible duration and nature of sickness.

DEGREE. Each Sign has 30° degrees and the 12 signs equal 360° Deg. Its mark is °. 60° is a Sextile ✶. 90° is a Square ▢. 120° is a Trine △. Each Degree is divided into 60′ Minutes and each Minute into 60″ Seconds.

DEGREE RISING AT BIRTH. The degree of the Zodiacal Sign posited on the Ascendant or cusp of the First House at birth. It is the most important point in the Nativity.

DESCENDANT. The cusp of the 7th House or western angle, opposite to the Ascendant.

DETRIMENT. When a Planet is in a Sign or House of an opposite nature to itself, or when placed in a Sign opposite to that of its own House and Sign, as Mars ♂ in Libra ♎.

DIGNITIES. A Planet in its own sign or house is most powerful, thus, Jupiter ♃ in Pisces ♓, Sagittarius ♐ or when ascending or culminating, is dignified.

DIRECTIONS. There are two Directions, primary and secondary. The Primary denote the

9

position of the Planets as life advances. The Sun ☉ moves about one degree a day, which is equivalent to one year Progressed. The thirtieth day after birth would denote the 30th year of life, and the Directions would be taken out of the Ephemeris for that day, the Sun's ☉ aspects forming the primary Directions, and the Moon the Secondary.

DIRECT MOTION. When the Planets are moving in their true order through the Zodiac, in the direction of the earth's annual revolution.

DISPOSITION. Indicated by the sign on the Ascendant and Planets in the first House.

Thus, Aries ♈ on the Ascendant would indicate that the native would be courageous, ambitious, ingenious, hasty and quick to take offence.

With Taurus ♉ rising, the native would be slow, plodding, patient, reserved, sympathetic, terrible in anger.

Gemini ♊, artistic, dual in nature, excitable, irritable, industrious and studious.

Cancer ♋, magnetic, affectionate, timid, distrustful.

Leo ♌, ambitious, pompous, faithful, liberal, determined.

Virgo ♍, industrious, capable, receptive—too much so—, kind and sensitive.

Libra ♎, gentle, fond of ease and pleasure, just and good tempered, fond of approbation.

Scorpio ♏, sarcastic, secretive, proud, contentious.

Sagittarius ♐, generous, philosophic, talkative, active, intellectual.

Capricorn ♑, ambitious, capricious, economic, diplomatic, cautious, melancholy.

Aquarius ♒, artistic, intuitive, refined, patient, expressive.

Pisces ♓, mediumistic, dualistic, thoughtful, sensitive, indolent, wary.

These must be considered first, then the planets in the Ascendant, then the ruler of the Ascendant, then the Planets in aspect to planets in the first House. It should be kept in mind that this is the key to the map and it requires careful study to render accurate judgment.

DRAGON'S HEAD (☊). The moon's ☽ North Node, or when she crosses the ecliptic into the North Latitude. The Moon ☽ is serpentine having a head and tail. Considered benefic, especially if in Taurus ♉.

DRAGON'S TAIL (☋). The Moon's ☽ South Node, when she crosses into the South Latitude. Considered Malific, the Dragon's Tail ☋ finds greatest joy in Scorpio ♏, the opposite of Taurus ♉.

DUMB SIGNS. See Mute.

11

DWA-DA-SHAMSA. A system for dividing each sign into twelve divisions of 2½ degrees each. These divisions being ruled by the Planets in the order of their rulership around the Zodiac. Thus the first 2½ degree division of the Sign is ruled by the ruler of that Sign, the second 2½ degrees by the ruler of the following sign, and so on, in their order around the circle. See bottom of page.

EARTH SIGNS. Taurus ♉, Virgo ♍, Capricorn ♑. These are considered cold and dry and govern the earthy, physical substance.

ECLIPSE. When a Planet partially or totally obscures the light of one Planet for another.

ECLIPTIC. The great circle in which the Sun ☉ appears to move annually. It is called the Ecliptic because eclipses generally take place

Divisions of				DWA-DA-
2½ Degrees each	1st	2nd	3rd	4th
Aries ♈ ....ruled by....	♂	♀	☿	☽
Taurus ♉ ....ruled by....	♀	☿	☽	☉
Gemini ♊ ....ruled by....	☿	☽	☉	☿
Cancer ♋ ....ruled by....	☽	☉	☿	♀
Leo ♌ ....ruled by....	☉	☿	♀	♂
Virgo ♍ ....ruled by....	☿	♀	♂	♃
Libra ♎ ....ruled by....	♀	♂	♃	♄
Scorpio ♏ ....ruled by....	♂	♃	♄	♄ ♅
Sagittarius ♐ ..ruled by....	♃	♄	♄ ♅	♃ ♆
Capricorn ♑ ....ruled by....	♄	♄ ♅	♃ ♆	♂
Aquarius ♒ ....ruled by....	♄ ♅	♃ ♆	♂	♀
Pisces ♓ ....ruled by....	♃ ♆	♂	♀	☿

when the Moon ☽ is on or near this circle. The Sun ☉ apparently makes a circuit through the Zodiac in one year.

ECLIPTIC TERRESTIAL. The path of the Moon ☽ in her course around the Earth.

ELECTION. The selection of a time to begin any new undertaking on which a figure is cast. A term used in Horary Astrology.

ELEVATED. The Planet nearest to the Mid-Heaven. The highest point in the Map.

EPHEMERIS. A tabulation of the Planets' places for each day in the year, giving Latitude, Longitude, Declinations, etc. Very necessary and important in casting a Horoscope.

EQUINOCTIAL SIGNS. Aries ♈, and Libra ♎, so called because the Sun enters these

SHAMSA

5th	6th	7th	8th	9th	10th	11th	12th
☉	☿	♀	♂	♃	♄	♄ ♅	♃ ♆
☿	♀	♂	♃	♄	♄ ♅	♃ ♆	♂
♀	♂	♃	♄	♄ ♅	♃ ♆	♂	♀
♂	♃	♄	♄ ♅	♃ ♆	♂	♀	☿
♃	♄	♄ ♅	♃ ♆	♂	♀	☿	☽
♄	♄ ♅	♃ ♆	♂	♀	☿	☽	☉
♄ ♅	♃ ♆	♂	♀	☿	☽	♋	☿
♃ ♆	♂	♀	☿	☽	♋	☿	♀
♂	♀	☿	☽	♋	☿	♀	♂
♀	☿	☽	♋	☿	♀	♂	♃
☽	♋	☿	♀	♂	♃	♄	♄ ♅

signs when transiting the Celestial Equator. When crossing the North Point in Aries ♈ it is termed the Vernal Equinox, and the South Point in Libra ♎ the Autumnal Equinox. At these periods the days and nights are of equal length.

ESSENTIAL DIGNITY. When a Planet is in its own Sign, or the Sign in which it finds its Exaltation.

EXALTATION. An Essential Dignity, next in power to that of the Planet's own house. The Sun ☉ is exalted in Aries ♈, Moon ☽ in Taurus ♉, Jupiter ♃ in Cancer ♋, Mercury ☿ in Virgo ♍, Saturn ♄ in Libra ♎, Mars ♂ in Capricorn ♑, and Venus ♀ in Pisces ♓. A Planet is essentially strong when in a Sign in which it is Exalted.

FALL. When a Planet is in a sign opposite to its exaltation, it is said to be in its "Fall" or weak.

FEMININE SIGNS. The even numbered signs, Taurus ♉, Cancer ♋, Virgo ♍, Scorpio ♏, Capricorn ♑, Pisces ♓. So called because they are receptive and negative in nature.

FIERY SIGNS. Aries ♈, Leo ♌, Sagittarius ♐. Also known as the Fiery Triplicity, and considered as the vital Signs.

FIGURE. A map of the Heavens erected from any given moment of time.

14

FIXED SIGNS. Tarus ♉, Leo ♌, Scorpio ♏ and Aquarius ♒. Their nature is fixed and immovable. They rule over the vital centres of the physical body.

Taurus ♉ rules the throat and is considered the most rigid of the fixed Signs. This Sign gives external will power, though under ordinary circumstances Taurus ♉ is negative and passive, but when aroused he is obstinate, unbending and stubborn.

Leo ♌ rules the heart and denotes the internal will guided by the heart and its motives.

Scorpio ♏ rules the generative organs and denotes the external will of action and reproduction.

Aquarius ♒ rules the blood and represents the will of expressed thought and motive.

It is important to note in what part of the body these Signs are placed for it shows that these matters will be fixed and unchangable. If the majority of Planets are found in fixed Signs at birth the character will be determined and steadfast and generally reliable. Either one of these Signs upon the Ascendant gives self-reliance, endurance and vitality, with power of concentration and good reasoning powers.

• FORTUNATE SIGNS. Aries ♈, Gemini ♊, Leo ♌, Libra ♎, Sagittarius ♐ and Aquarius ♒

are considered most fortunate when on the Ascendant for the reason that they are positive Signs.

FORTUNES. Jupiter ♃, Venus ♀, the Sun ☉ and Mercury ☿ when well placed.

FRUITFUL SIGNS. Cancer ♋, Scorpio ♏, Pisces ♓. The water triplicity.

GEMINI (♊). The Twins. The third sign or House of Mercury ☿. It is dual, double bodied, and positive. The Sun ☉ enters this Sign on May 22.

GENETHLIACAL. That which deals with the geniture in a Nativity. Natal Astrology.

GEOCENTRIC. A system of Astrology in which the Earth is considered as the center of the universe. Heliocentric Astrology pertains to the conditions of the Earth as viewed from the Sun ☉ as the center.

GIVER OF LIFE. The Sun ☉ is often considered as the giver of life in a male nativity.

HEALTH. Ruled largely by the Sign Ascending, indicating the parts of the physical body most vital or sensitive, also the nature of complaints the Native is most liable to. Look also to the Sign on the cusp of the 6th House and the Planets in the 1st and 6th. The Sun ☉ and Moon ☽ under good aspects will give strength to the constitution, but when afflicted will indicate poor health and frequent sickness.

16

HELEOCENTRIC. Taking the Sun ⊙ as the center.

HERMAPHRODITE. Dual sexed—male and female. A term also applied to Mercury ☿ owing to his dual nature.

HERSHALL. A name sometimes applied to the Planet Uranus ♅, the discoverer of the Planet.

HORARY. From the latin word Hora, meaning an hour.

HORARY ASTROLOGY. A system utilized in the solution of questions of importance, based upon a figure or map, cast at the moment the question is asked.

HOUSES. The 12 divisions of the Zodiac and their influence, as follows:

First House. Early environment, childhood, personal appearance.

Second House. Wealth and financial standing. What we earn and what we make of it.

Third House. Short journeys. Brothers and sisters. Neighbors. Writings.

Fourth House. The father. Old age. Inheritance. Removals. Houses and land. Also the condition and position of native at close of life.

Fifth House. Children. Love. Courtship. Messengers, Amusements, Newspapers. Success in speculation and hazard.

Sixth House. Health. The diseases that native is most liable to. Servants, uncles and aunts.

Seventh House. Marriage. Partnership. Lawsuits. Public enemies. Rivals.

Eighth House. Death. Wills. Legacies. The estate or dowry of the wife or husband.

Ninth House. The mind. Religion. Dreams and visions. Long journeys. Sea voyages.

Tenth House. Social standing. Honor. Trade or profession.

Eleventh House. Friends. Hopes. Wishes. Wealth of mother.

Twelfth House. Sorrow and self undoing. Secret enemies. Assaults on person. Imprisonment.

HUMANE SIGNS. Gemini ♊, Virgo ♍, Aquarius ♒, the first half of Sagittarius ♐ and Pisces ♓. These signs on the Ascendant give the Native a humane disposition, especially if the Ruler be in one of them.

HYLEG. Signifies the Giver of Life. The Sun ☉, Moon ☽, and Ascendant.

INCREASING IN LIGHT. When the Moon ☽ or any Planet is leaving the Sun ☉ until the opposition is reached. When a Planet, and especially the Moon ☽, is increasing in light the influence is good, but unfortunate when decreasing.

INFERIOR PLANETS. The Moon ☽, Mercury ☿, and Venus ♀. So called because their orbit is inferior to that of the Earth.

INFORTUNES. Saturn ♄, Mars ♂, Uranus ♅, also Neptune ♆ when afflicted.

INTERCEPTED SIGNS. A sign lying between the Cusp of two Houses.

JUPITER. The Greater Fortune. The Largest Planet in our Solar System. Has a period of 11 years 314 days 12 hours. Daily motion, 5'

LATITUDE. The distance of a Planet or star North or South of the Ecliptic.

LEO (♌). The Lion. The fifth sign of the Zodiac. Fixed, sterile, fiery, masculine. Rules the heart. Home of the Sun. The Sun enters this Sign on July 23rd.

LIBRA (♎). The Scales. The 7th Sign of the Zodiac. House of Venus ♀. Cardinal, air Sign, restless, judicial. The Sun ☉ enters this Sign on Sept. 24th.

LIGHTS. Refer to the Sun ☉ and Moon ☽.

LONGITUDE. Refers to any place east or west of Greenwich. Also the distance of any star or planet from the first point of the Zodiac as measured on the ecliptic.

LORD. The ruler of a Sign or House. Mars ♂ is the Lord of Aries ♈ and if Aries ♈ is on the Ascendant it would be Lord, or ruler of the Ascendant.

LUMINARIES. The Sun ☉ or Moon ☽.

LUNATION. A Lunar period. The length of time in which the Moon ☽ appears to move around the Earth, or the time elapsed from New Moon ☽ to New Moon. This term is also used to signify the different aspects of the Moon ☽ to the Sun ☉ as the Conjunction ☌, Square □, or Opposition ☍.

MALIFICS. Saturn ♄ and Mars ♂. Also Mercury ☿ when associated with malifics manifests an evil influence. Uranus ♅ under certain conditions, when the Native is unawakened.

MARS. The Planet Mars has a period of 1 year 321 days 22 hours. A diurnal motion of 31'. He is retrograde for 80 days, and 2 days stationary before and after.

MASCULINE PLANETS. Sun ♒, Mars ♂, Jupiter ♃, and Saturn ♄.

MASCULINE SIGNS. Aries ♈, Gemini ♊, Leo ♌, Libra ♎, Sagittarius ♐, Aquarius ♒. The odd signs of the Zodiac.

MEAN MOTION. The daily movement of a Planet.

MERCURY. The Planet Mercury is never more than 30° from the Sun. Has a period of 87 days 23 hours, and a mean motion of about 3° degrees. Mercury is retrograde for 24 days and stationary 1 day.

MERIDIAN. The circle crossing the Equator at right angles from the Poles. Every place has its own Meridian.

MID-HEAVEN. The 10th House.

MOON. The Satellite of the Earth, revolves in an elliptical orbit around the Earth in 27 days 7 hours 43 minutes and 11 seconds. (To 29 days 12 hours) its mean daily motion is 12° 15'. It is said to be 240,000 miles from the earth.

MOVABLE SIGNS. Aries ♈, Cancer ♋, Libra ♎, Capricorn ♑. The Sun ☉ passes from one season to another when passing through these signs.

MUNDANE ASPECTS. The distance upon the earth when measured by the Semi-Arc, taking no notice of intercepted signs and counting each House as containing 30° degrees.

MUTE SIGNS. Cancer ♋, Scorpio ♏, Pisces ♓. The water triplicity.

NADIR, or Immum Coeli—usually written I. C. The fourth House in the Horoscope.

NATIVITY. The Birth figure of an Individual drawn for the moment of birth.

NEPTUNE. The most distant Planet of our Solar System. Was discovered in 1846. It has a cycle of 165 years.

NODES. Also called the Dragon's Head ☊ and Tail ☋, (which see.)

NORTHERN SIGNS. Aries ♈, Taurus ♉, Gemini ♊, Cancer ♋, Leo ♌, and Virgo ♍.

OCCIDENTAL. The western portion of the map.

OPPOSITION. When two Planets are 180° degrees apart they are in opposition ☍. This aspect is usually considered malific.

ORB. The orbs of the Planets are the number of degrees allowed to each, in which their influence is felt. Five degrees each way is considered the safest number, and one degree each way in Progression. This influence is strongest when applying.

ORIENTAL. When a Planet is in the Eastern part of the figure between the 4th and 10th houses it is Oriental.

PARALLEL. The Declination North or South of the Equator. It has the same nature as a Conjunction ♂, only more powerful and effective. The Parellel of the Sun ☉ and Jupiter ♃ is considered good, while the Sun ☉ and Satuhn ♄ is evil. With Planets of a benefic nature the influence is good if well aspected.

PART OF FORTUNE (⊕). A point in the Horoscope where the rays of the Sun ☉ and Moon ☽ converge. The method of computing this is explained in the "Instructions" given in "Technique of Astrology." Its Influence applies to material gain.

PISCES (♓). The Fishes. The 12th sign of the Zodiac, ruled by Jupiter ♃ and Neptune ♆, which have great power when in this Sign. It is moist, cold, negative, watery, phlegmatic, effeminate, nocturnal, and bicorporeal. The Sun ☉ enters this sign on Feb. 21st.

PLANETARY HOURS. The Planets have dominion over the days of the week, as follows:

Sunday ☉. The Sun's day.

Monday ☽. The Moon's day.

Tuesday ♂. The day of the Norse God **Tyr**, corresponding to Mars.

Wednesday ☿. The day of the Norse God Wodin, Wotan, or Mercury.

Thursday ♃. The day of the Norse God Thor, or Jupiter.

Friday ♀. The day of the Norse God **Freya,** or Venus.

Saturday ♄. Saturn's day.

The Planets also have special dominion in turns over the Sunrise hour of their day and repeat throughout the day in the following orderly sequence. See the Planetary Hour Dial for the sunrise hour throughout the year.

Sunday ⊙	♀	☿	☽	♄	♃	♂
Monday ☽	♄	♃	♂	⊙	♀	☿
Tuesday ♂	⊙	♀	☿	☽	♄	♃
Wednesday ☿	☽	♄	♃	♂	⊙	♀
Thursday ♃	♂	⊙	♀	☿	☽	♄
Friday ♀	☿	☽	♄	♃	♂	⊙
Saturday ♄	♃	♂	⊙	♀	☿	☽

*The Planetary Hour Dial. The Simplex Publishing Co.

QUARTILE (□), or Square. When two Planets are 90° degrees apart. Considered an unfavorable aspect.

QUERANT. One who asks a Horary question.

QUINTILE (Q). Two Planets 72° apart. An inferior Aspect, seldom used.

RADICAL POSITIONS. The Degree and Minute of a Planet in the natal Horoscope.

RADIX. The Natal Horoscope.

RECEPTION. The Planet that receives the Aspect.

RECTIFICATION. A method by which the true time of birth is discovered, when unknown.

It is most important to have the exact moment of birth in casting a Horoscope figure.

RETROGRADE (℞). A Planet which is apparently decreasing in Longitude. It also indicates that the Planet is weak or debilitated.

REVOLUTIONS. The return of the Sun ☉ or other Planet to its radical place at birth.

RIGHT ASCENSION. The Arc of the Equator reckoned from the first minute of Aries ♈.

RULER. That Planet which has greatest dominion and influence over the life of the Native. Other things being equal, the Lord of the Ascendant is the Ruler.

SAGITTARIUS (♐). The Archer. The 9th sign of the Zodiac. It is hot, dry, choleric, masculine, eastern, common, bicoporial, changeable, southern, obeying. Home of Jupiter ♃. The Sun ☉ enters this sign on Nov. 23rd.

SATURN. The Planet Saturn completes the circuit around the Earth in 29 years 167 days, 5 hours, with a mean motion of 2' per day. He is retrograde for 140 days, stationary 5 days before and after.

SCORPIO (♏). The Scorpion. The 8th sign of the Zodiac. It is fixed, mute, nocturnal, cold, moist, watery, phlegmatic, feminine, southern. Rules the generative organs, and one of the most fruitful signs. Home of Mars ♂. The Sun ☉ enters Scorpio ♏ on Oct. 24th.

SEMI-SEXTILE (⚹). A difference of 30° in Longitude. A good aspect but weak.

SEMI-SQUARE   (∟). An   aspect of 45°
in Longitude. Considered evil.

SESQUI-QUADRATE (S.Q.). An evil minor
aspect, being a difference of 135° degrees in
Longitude.

SEXTILE (✱). When two or more Planets
are 60° degrees apart in the Zodiac. A good
aspect.

SIDERIAL TIME. The true right Ascension
on the Meridian at noon. The angular distance
of the first point of Aries ♈, or the true Vernal
Equinox.

SIGNIFICATOR. The ruling Planet of the
Ascendant.

SIGNS OF LONG ASCENSION. Cancer ♋,
Leo ♌, Virgo ♍, Libra ♎, Scorpio ♏ and Sagittarius ♐. So called because they take a longer
time passing over the Ascendant.

SIGNS OF SHORT ASCENSION. Aries ♈,
Taurus ♉, Gemini ♊, Capricorn ♑, Aquarius ♒,
Pisces ♓. So called because they take a shorter
period in passing over the Ascendant.

SIGNS OF VOICE. Gemini ♊, Libra ♎, the
latter part of Virgo ♍, and the first part of Sagittarius ♐. When any of these are found on
the Ascendant with Mercury ☿ and the Moon ☽
in good position and unafflicted, the native will
be a good speaker or orator.

SIGNS. The twelve signs of the Zodiac and
their Rulers. (See first three columns).

Planets are said to Rule or to be essentially
Dignified in the following signs (see column
"Ruler") in the following table.

Planets are more powerful in the following signs (see Exaltation) or when occupying the opposite signs, they are in their Fall (see 3rd column).

	Ruler	Exaltation	Fall	Detriment
Aries ♈ the Ram	♂	☉	♄	♀
Taurus ♉ the Bull	♀	☽	♅	♂
Gemini ♊ the Twins	☿	....	....	♃
Cancer ♋ the Crab	☽	♃ ♆	♂	♄
Leo ♌ the Lion	☉	....	☿	♄ ♅
Virgo ♍ the Virgin	☿	☿	♀	♃ ♆
Libra ♎ the Scales	♀	♄	☉	♂
Scorpio ♏ the Scorpion	♂	♅	☽	♀
Sagittarius ♐ the Archer	♃	....	....	☿
Capricorn ♑ the Goat	♄	♂	♃ ♆	☽
Aquarius ♒ the Waterman	♄ ♅	....	....	☉
Pisces ♓ the Fishes	♃ ♆	♀	☿	☿

When a Planet is within orb of 3 degrees in the following Points it is considered a critical degree:

Cardinal	1° 13° & 26°	of	♈	♋	♎	♑
Fixed	= 9° & 21°	of	♉	♌	♏	♒
Common	4° 17°	of	♊	♍	♐	♓

SOUTHERN SIGNS. Libra ♎, Scorpio ♏, Sagittarius ♐, Capricorn ♑, Aquarius ♒, Pisces ♓.

SPECULUM. A table of the Aspects in the Horoscope.

SQUARE. When two Planets are 90° Degrees apart, they are said to be Square □ or Quartile. This Aspect is said to be bad.

STATIONARY. When a Planet is stationary and appears to have no motion, as when changing from Retrograde ℞ to Direct D, or the reverse, it is said to be stationary.

SUCCEEDANT HOUSES. Those Houses which follow the angles. The 2nd, 5th, 8th and 11th.

SUPERIOR PLANETS. Neptune ♆, Uranus ♅, Saturn ♄, Jupiter ♃ and Mars ♂. So named because they are superior to the Earth and beyond it from the Sun ☉. The inferior Planets Venus ♀ and Mercury ☿ are between the Earth and the Sun ☉, they are also inferior in size and in their influence. The superior Planets are much more powerful in their aspects and direction and their influence lasts longer.

SUN. The center of our Planetary System. The Earth revolves around the Sun in 365 days 5 hours 49 minutes and 49 seconds. Mean daily motion 59′ 0″.

SYMBOLS OF THE PLANETS:

The Sun ☉—A circle with a dot in the center.

The Moon ☽—A half circle.

Mars ♂—The circle with a cross above.

Venus ♀—The circle with a cross below.

Saturn ♄—A half circle with the cross above.

Jupiter ♃—A half circle with the cross below.

Mercury ☿—The circle, the half circle and the cross.

27

These symbols are highly significant, and the Student is advised to read "Simplified Scientific Astrology," page 165-8 for the best interpretation.

TABLE OF HOUSES. A table showing the Degree and Minute of the different Signs on the twelve Houses. Used in calculating a Nativity.

TAURUS (♉). The Bull. The second Sign of the Zodiac. Home of Venus ♀. Taurus ♉ is of the Earth Triplicity, feminine, nocturnal, fixed, cold, dry, melancholy. The nature of this sign corresponds to the nature of the Bull. The Sun ☉ enters Taurus ♉ on April 22nd.

TRANSITS. The position of the Planets in the Horoscope at birth constitute the "Radix" or root of all action. The passage of any Planet over this position is called a Transit and these Transits are highly important in connection with "Progressed" readings. Especial attention should be paid to where the Aspect takes place in the chart.

TRINE (△). When two Planets are 120° apart. A good aspect.

TRIPLICITY. The twelve Signs are divided into Trigons or Triplicities, corresponding to the four elements, as follows: Fire—Aries ♈, Leo♌, Sagittarius ♐. Air—Gemini ♊, Libra ♎, Aquarius ♒. Water—Cancer ♋, Scorpio ♏, Pisces ♓. Earth—Taurus ♉, Virgo ♍, Capricorn ♑.

URANUS, discovered in 1781. Makes a complete circuit of our Planetary System in approximately 83 years 273 days 8 hours, with a mean daily mation of 3″.

28

VENUS. The Planet Venus revolves around the Earth in 224 days 17 hours and has a mean motion of 72′. It is retrograde for 42 days and stationary 2 days before and after.

VIRGO (♍). The Virgin. The 6th sign of the Zodiac. House of Mercury☿. It is feminine, critical, practical, helpful, an Earth sign. The Sun ☉ enters Virgo ♍ on Aug. 23rd.

VIOLENT SIGNS. Aries ♈, Libra ♎, Scorpio ♏, Capricorn ♑ and Aquarius ♒. These signs are the Houses of the Malific Planets. Taurus ♉ and Leo ♌ are also considered of a violent nature.

WATER SIGNS. Cancer ♋, Scorpio ♏, and Pisces ♓ are called the Water Signs.

ZENITH. The Highest Point in the heavens above the birthplace.

ZODIAC. A narrow Belt of the Heavens containing the twelve Signs of the Zodiac.

ZODIACAL CONSTELLATIONS are as follows. Each sign governs that part of the body named.

	Sign	House	Governs
Aries, (the Ram)	♈	1st	Head and face
Taurus, (the Bull	♉	2nd	Neck, throat, ears
Gemini, (the Twins)	♊	3rd	Arms, shoulders
Cancer, (the Crab)	♋	4th	Breast, stomach
Leo, (the Lion)	♌	5th	Back and heart

Virgo,
(the Virgin) ....♍ 6th—Belly and uterus
Libra,
(the Scales) ....♎ 7th—Kidneys and loins
Scorpio,
(the Scorpion) ....♏ 8th—Sex organs, rectum
Sagittarius,
(the Archer) ....♐ 9th—Thighs and hips
Capricorn,
(the Goat) ....♑ 10th—The knees
Aquarius,
(the Waterbearer) ♒ 11th—Calves and ankles
Pisces,
(the Fishes ....♓ 12th—The Feet

It is important to note what part of the Body these signs are placed, for it shows that these matters will be fixed and unchangeable. If the majority of Planets are found to be in Fixed Signs at birth, the character is determined, Steadfast and generally reliable: either one of the fixed signs upon the Ascendant gives self reliance, endurance and vitality, with powers of concentration and good reasoning faculties.

.

www.ingramcontent.com/pod-product-compliance
Lightning Source LLC
Chambersburg PA
CBHW031617040426
42452CB00006B/563

* 9 7 8 1 4 3 4 4 7 0 1 4 0 *